Contents

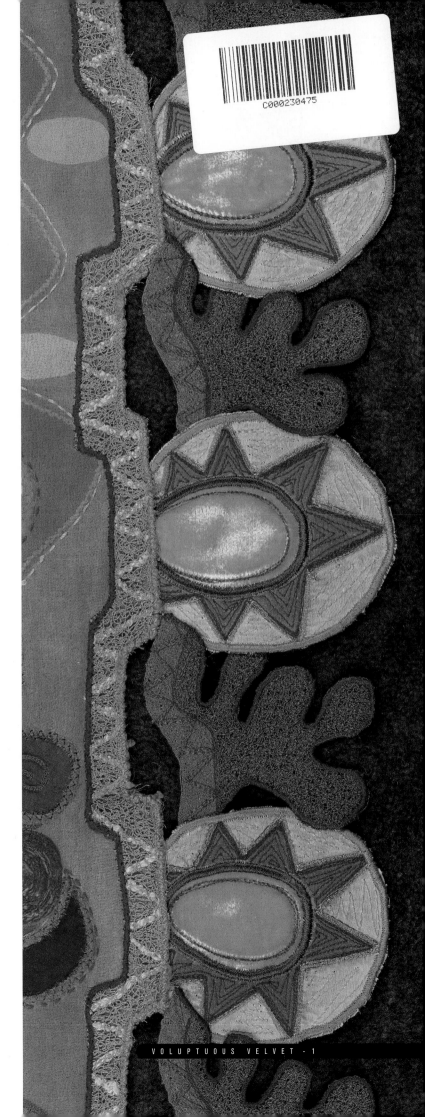

Introduction   2

Adding Colour - Natural fibres   4

Useful Equipment   5

Printed Velvet Samples   6

Adding Colour - Synthetics   8

Discharge Methods   9

Discharge With Colour   10

Devoré   12

Burning the Pile   14

Bonding & Appliqué   16

Stitching to Enrich   18

Suppliers   22

Additional Reading   22

And Finally...   24

*Cover: Karen E MacPherson -
'The Chameleon Touch'
Procion dye in manutex paste painted
onto silk viscose velvet with machine
stitching, supported on a ground
fabric with a layer of thin wadding.*

*Left: 'Letter From Turkey' (detail)
A variety of synthetic velvets ironed
onto bondaweb - cut and applied to
dyed handmade paper, enriched
with hand and machine stitching.*

Introduction to
Voluptuous Velvet

Velvet has always been viewed as a luxury fabric associated with richness and wealth and can be made from a number of natural and synthetic fibres. It has often been reserved for special ritualistic occasions and goes in and out of fashion. At present, it is enjoying a high profile with a huge range of fibres, colours and textures. It makes a statement, feels gorgeous and can be fashioned into wondrous garments and furnishings.

Because it has such a strong and compelling surface, using it sympathetically in embroideries can be a challenge.

At this point be warned - working with velvet can become addictive. The lustrous array of colours and textures lure the unguarded into impulse buys which sit temptingly on a shelf waiting for just the right occasion. As with most fabrics, sample first before buying in any quantity.

What should you collect? Every type you can find is the answer, for each has its own characteristics. You will need to experiment to find the velvets which work best for you. A rummage through most ragbags or jumble sales will reveal old faded velvet curtains, clothes and other items which may be cannibalised and utilised. These will not always have labels and so it is necessary to feel the fabrics and become used to the subtle differences in order to determine their composition. One of my most useful finds has been cotton panne velvet, taken from a nineteen-thirties wedding dress which I have dyed and manipulated using every last scrap because of its beautiful surface texture.

You will come across silk, cotton, viscose, synthetic or mixes. Each has a unique feel and is capable of being adapted and altered in a number of ways. Knowing the composition will help you to work out the most appropriate way of dealing with it. While the silk velvets feel luscious and dye beautifully, the synthetics should not be dismissed as they can be coloured and distressed into richly textured surfaces. Pale colours are particularly useful for dying.

I hope, by using some of the techniques in this book, that you will learn to enjoy and develop a fascination for velvet.

Right: Velvet Pincushions
The pincushions demonstrate the techniques highlighted in the book and include a range of dyeing methods, free bonding and appliqué with hand and machine stitching.

Adding Colour to Natural Fibres

This can be best achieved by using cream, white or pale coloured silk cotton or viscose velvets. As with other fabrics, darker colours are more difficult to change except by discharge methods (see page 9).

There are no universal dyes which are successful on all types of fabric. However, with natural fibres which are cellulose based such as cotton, viscose and rayon, Procion dyes work well. These are available from many suppliers and can be bought ready prepared for dyeing. A thickener such as Manutex can be mixed with the Procion for printing and painting directly onto fabric.

• For silk velvets, acid dyes give vibrant results.
• Direct dyes work well on all natural fibres.
• Silk paints may be used on natural fibres but may flatten the pile of velvet. Silk paints applied to a wet fabric will bleed and blend more easily. After fixing with the iron and a gentle wash, the pile may be revived with steam or a velvet pressing mat. The use of these dyes and fabric paints are well illustrated in numerous books so the following points are simple guidelines.
• Washing machine dyes, available in most large stores, work very well for large pieces of cotton velvet where flat colour is required.

• Procion dyes available from specialist suppliers can be sprinkled or sprayed onto the surface of fabrics and combined with fixatives for colourful results. Always be careful when using Procion dyes to wear gloves and a mask.
• Once the base colour has been applied, further colours may be achieved by printing or stencilling spraying and other patterning methods.
• Where fabric paints have been applied to the surface, it is usually better to dry flat as the colour can bleed down the fabric if hung.

If a fabric is to be used for clothing then all manufacturer's instructions for fixing should be carefully followed.

It should also be born in mind that direct sunlight should be avoided for any dyed fabric, as this would fade even professionally prepared curtain fabrics.

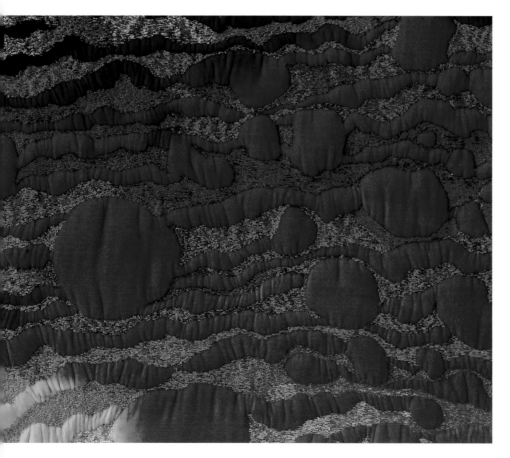

Karen E MacPherson - Velvet Sample
Silk viscose velvet painted with procion dye in Manutex. The free machining is worked on the velvet supported on a background with light wadding to emphasise the distortion.

Useful Equipment

Many of us desire professional effects but only have access to domestic and easily available materials. With this in mind, illustrated here are some basic items which have proved to be useful.

• The most effective printing surface I have discovered is an ironing sheet (foam-backed,metallic surface). For wooden block and other flat printing materials, it allows just the right amount of flexibility for a successful print.
• Protective gloves, protective eye wear (when using bleach) and a mask for noxious substances are a sensible precaution.

• Collect a variety of printing materials such as blocks, stencils, plastic lace mats and paper doilies, plant materials, leaves and ferns, corks and foam sponge which may be used for texture or cut into shapes.
• Paint brushes for applying dye need not be the most expensive and some excellent sponge applicators are available from good children's shops. A plastic palette knife is very useful, as is an old toothbrush.
• A simple silk screen with fine terylene stretched over a home-made wooden frame and stapled on is quite sufficient. The screen is masked off with masking tape. Professional squeegees are available in art shops but a window cleaning squeegee blade is a cheaper substitute. Although not essential, very useful for delivering devoré paste.

• Masking tape for holding down the fabric will help accuracy.
• Paper towel is useful for keeping everything clean and avoiding spots of bleach or paste which will ruin the print.
• Thick household bleach works well for discharge but USE WITH CARE. Plastic dispensers with a nozzle make it easier to manage. Hairdressers often discard useful bottles which are ideal.
• JACQUARD DISCHARGE PASTE and FIBER-ETCH are both useful commercial products,specifically designed for techniques described in this book.
• TRANSFER paints are excellent for colouring synthetic velvet and prove very effective when printed, overprinted or discharged.

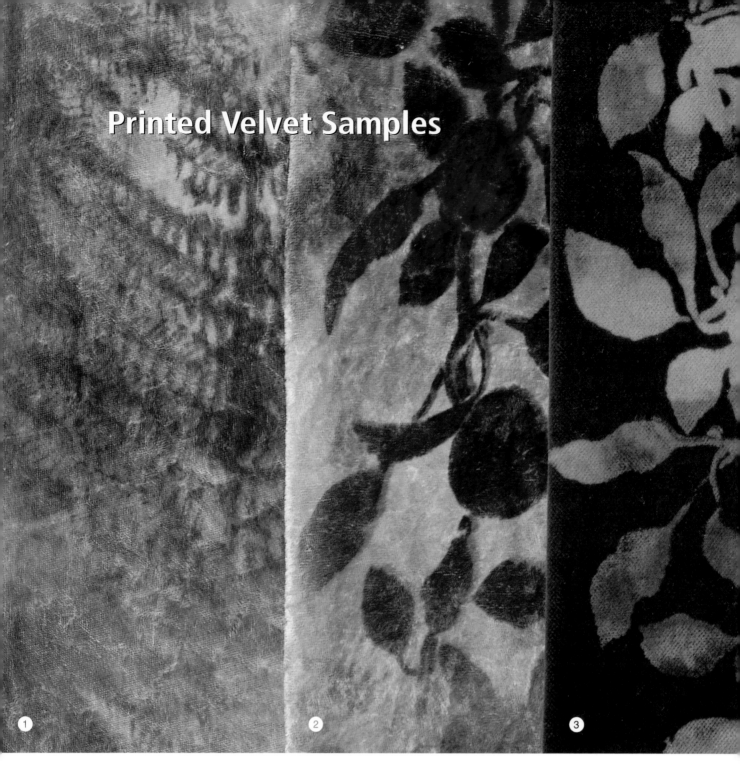

Printed Velvet Samples

❶ White synthetic velvet with fern prints and overprinting using transfer prints.

❷ Synthetic velvet with a random sponge transfer paint and overprinted with stencilled patterns.

❸ Cotton velvet with thick bleach sponged through a stencil. The colour variation occurs as the sponge dries out of bleach in repeated prints (be careful not to flood the sponge).

❹ Cotton velvet with plastic tablecloth used as a stencil for bleach.

❺ Discharge cotton velvet with discharge paste mixed with pigment and painted onto wooden printing block.

❻ Coloured synthetic velvet with a variety of transfer paint prints.

Adding Colour - Synthetics

There are numerous synthetic velvets available, many of them stretchy, which can be successfully incorporated into embroidered surfaces.

Transfer paints give very good results with synthetic and mixed fibres and velvet has an extra dimension of piled surface.

Light to medium tones will produce the most colourful effects but mid tones can be altered to produce rich and ornate colours and patterns which disguise the humble origins of the fabric.

Points to remember:
• Transfer paints are applied to paper and then ironed onto fabric.
• The paper should be thin and fairly non-absorbent such as photocopy, typing or layout pad.
• Apply the transfer paint with a sponge or any printing material. (see pages 6 & 7).
• Allow to dry thoroughly before ironing off.
• Test the velvet first as some can scorch easily. If in doubt, use baking parchment over the transfer paper to diffuse the heat.
• It is best to use a flat iron as the holes of a steam iron can impress onto the pattern.

• Iron onto the velvet, moving the iron easily over the surface, ensuring that all the edges are ironed off and there are no missing areas.

Try overprinting layers for atmospheric and abstract effects. Start with lighter coloured prints first and build up.

The paper may be DISCHARGED with thick bleach, printed, painted or applied with a plastic applicator. ALLOW TO DRY THOROUGHLY before ironing off and iron outside, or in a well-ventilated space or wear a mask. This technique has the advantages of a discharged look without the fabric itself being affected.

Using a combination of the above, even the most lurid colours may be altered into stunning patterns and these can be further adapted by burning (see page 16).

Velvet Book Cover
The book is displayed against the bright pink synthetic velvet which was used as a base fabric before transfer paints. On pink, the yellow throws up magical vibrant oranges and when ironing off onto coloured synthetics, the base colour must be taken into consideration as it will affect the colours. The cover displays the discharge method where bleach has been applied to the paper to discharge the colour in heart shapes before drying and ironing off.

Discharge - Removing Colour from Velvets

Cotton and silk velvets can be used to good effect for discharge with bleach and discharge paste. Professionally or home dyed DARK colours work particularly well. There is a professionally dyed black discharge velvet available which is specially designed for the purpose and produces excellent effects. Furnishing velvets can also prove useful if they have not been treated with a protective coating. Velvet upholstery samples books are particularly desirable.

Viscose velvets work with bleach although the results can be unpredictable. However, good 'antiqued' effects can be further enhanced by burning and this is not so successful with the natural fibres. Viscose velvet does not react well to the discharge paste.

Before beginning we should remember that bleach and the discharge paste are hazardous materials so take the recommended precautions and cover up, wear gloves, work in a well ventilated space and avoid inhaling the fumes or wear a mask. Spots of bleach on clothing can be very annoying.

Bleach

Thick, domestic bleach available from supermarkets works well as it is more controllable than thin bleach. It can be painted, sponged, printed, stencilled and used in any of the ways described in pages 6 and 7, but it needs careful handling both from the safety point of view and to achieve the right effects.

Useful hints when using bleach
• Plastic bottles with nozzles are useful for drawing on fabric.
• Avoid drips falling in unplanned areas, particularly when using printing blocks. It is better to paint or sponge the bleach onto the printing block than to dip it in as this is easier to control.
• Allow to dry thoroughly and be prepared for it to remain active albeit at a declining rate as long as it is even slightly wet.
• Rinse in vinegar (acetic acid) to neutralise the bleach and prevent rotting. Although this technique has been disputed, I have used it for many years and so far no rotting has occurred. However, I would advise against exposing the resulting piece to prolonged direct sunlight.
• Using water will only reactivate and dilute the bleach but, after the vinegar, the fabric may be washed. When neutralised and washed, the fabric may be flooded with silk paints, etc. and overprinted for more complicated imagery.
• Bleach can be mixed with a thickener such as Manutex for painting, printing and using with a silk screen.

Discharge Paste

This paste is specifically designed for discharge and can be bought from specialist outlets. It must be used in a well-ventilated area as it smells dreadful but has the advantage of being the ideal consistency for printing.

The discharge process takes place with heat and so when printing or painting it is difficult to ascertain the final effect but this adds interest to the process. Allow to dry or dry with a hair drier and iron with a steam iron to expose the exciting results.

Stencilled patterning achieved with bleach on to cotton discharge velvet through a plastic stencil

Discharge with Colour

The discharge paste has another great advantage as it can be used with colour, making it possible for the process of colour removal and adding colour to happen simultaneously. This provides the ideal answer for those who wish to dye dark colours with lighter ones. It is designed for natural fibres.

Most colouring agents and fabric paints can be used to varying effect. Experiment on small areas and use ends of bottles of silk or permanent paint that you may have in your work box.

The most vigorous results are gained when using pigment colour in with the paste. Small quantities of pigment give good depth of colour and allow the paste to exert its full effect.

Silk paints need to be used in greater proportion to achieve any depth of colour but too much dilutes the paste and reduces its efficacy. As a rough guide, one third silk paint to two thirds paste gives adequate, if subtle results.

Book cover on discharged cloth

The background cloth of black cotton velvet was discharged with bleach printed with a cut foam block. When dry, the cloth was neutralised with vinegar then rinsed clean. Silk paint was flooded into the velvet and ironed to fix. The cloth was then washed again. The book cover was printed with discharge paste mixed with silk paint which has the advantage of taking the black out and putting the colour in the same operation.

The iridescent highlights were achieved by applying spots of P.V.A. glue which was allowed to become 'tacky' and 'Transfoil' burnished over.The glue picks up the foil to enhance the print.

Joanna O'Neill - Wall Hanging Black discharge cotton with discharge paste and pigment printed with sponge blocks. This was enriched with further gold printing and hand stitch.

Devoré

Devoré has enjoyed great popularity in recent years. It produces a seductive cloth which involves a careful technique. It is not therefore surprising to find that scarves and clothes incorporating devoré are expensive.

Devoré velvet is worked on a mixed fibre ground of which silk viscose is the most readily available. It works by chemically 'burning' the pile and leaving the ground fabric intact. This is a relatively expensive fabric so experiment with very small pieces as it takes practice to achieve good results.

There are various recipes which involve suspending chemicals in a paste which is then applied to the back of the velvet. Having experimented with various pastes, I have achieved the most reliable results with 'FIBER-ETCH' which is available from specialist outlets.

Useful hints for working devoré
• The best and most reliable results are undoubtedly gained using silk screen to deliver the paste. This need not be complicated as a simple wooden frame with tautly stretched fine terylene masked with masking tape will be sufficient.
• 'FIBER-ETCH' delivered by silk screen works well for small areas but would be expensive for large lengths.
• The paste may also be applied with sponge or brush or from the dispenser nozzle.
• BE CAREFUL not to flood the paste as it can eat through the pile AND the ground if over-generous.
• Use a clean surface with paper towel underneath.
• Hold the fabric secure with masking tape.
• Apply paste to the REVERSE of the fabric.
• Dry with a hair drier or allow to dry.
• Use clean paper towel, turn fabric over and iron the PILE side using WOOL setting in a well ventilated area or wear a mask.
• The paste chemically 'burns' the cellulose fibres and will have a singed appearance so do not worry when it looks charred. If too much paste has been applied, it can 'burn' right through.
• Rinse the resulting cloth under a cold tap and gently ease the pile off the ground.
• Wash thoroughly.
• Allow to dry.

NB: Remember that accurate patterns are very difficult on a small scale and it takes time to gain expertise in this technique so keep samples with notes.

Now it may be coloured in any appropriate technique such as dip dye or surface sprinkle method. Procion dyes give good depth of colour but the silk ground will dye a paler shade.

'FIBER-ETCH' was delivered onto the reverse of the silk viscose velvet by means of silk screen. The pattern was achieved by painting P.V.A. triangles onto the mesh to resist the paste. After 'burning' off the fibres and washing and drying the velvet, Procion dye mixed with salt was sprinkled on the fabric, and water mixed with washing soda, sprayed through a plant spray to spread and fix the colour. After half an hour, the fabric was rinsed clean under a cold tap.

Burning the Pile

This technique is most effective with synthetic and viscose velvets which respond to heat. The pile can be burned in numerous ways but the most safe and effective is a soldering tool. Domestic soldering irons are quite adequate but there are specialist pyrography and craft soldering irons available.

There are two basic methods and the first is best worked in a frame.

Method 1
• Frame up the velvet and burn through the pile and/or ground to the desired pattern and texture. This technique has the advantage of sealing the edge to prevent fray.
• By holding the soldering iron at an angle to the surface it is possible to carve and sculpt the surface.
• Try two contrasting synthetic velvets and carve through the upper layer to reveal the under colour.
• Make a variety of scored marks.
• Apply further layers to the surface and fuse with the heat.
• Always work in a well ventilated space or wear a mask.

Method 2
• Pyrography irons are sold with a variety of ends which 'brand' marks into the surface.
• Place the fabric on a metal tin lid or similar.
• Press heated tool into the surface and against the metal to indent patterns.
• The resulting fabric can have a stiff effect where the melted fibres accumulate.
• Use several layers and fabric mixes for more exotic surfaces.

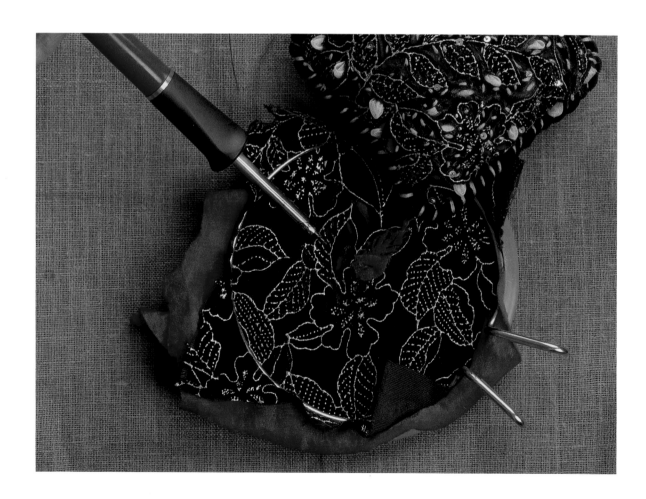

*Chrissy Hillier - Fabric Sample
Synthetic velvet burned with a
soldering iron, placed on a
contrasting fabric and stitched
with herringbone stitch.*

Bonding & Appliqué

Bonding and appliqué are conventional methods of decorating and enriching a cloth but there are some variations which can be used very successfully with velvet.

Using Bondaweb
Bondaweb can be most useful but be aware of the quality of the cloth.
Synthetics can burn under the iron so always test first and if in doubt place baking parchment over the fabric to diffuse the heat.

Thin synthetic velvets can be applied easily to each other or to contrasting fabrics but thick velvets are difficult to use as the heat does not penetrate the pile. For thicker fabrics, conventional appliqué should be used. Bondaweb can be useful in preventing fraying.

Possibilities
• Iron Bondaweb onto the reverse of the velvet, cut into the desired shape, remove paper, place sticky side down onto fabric surface and iron (with baking parchment over if necessary).
• Remove web from the ground and place directly onto the surface in desired shape. Chop and tear fragments onto the web. (Try mixing velvet with lace scraps, etc.) Place baking parchment over the top and iron. It needs further stitching to secure the pieces.
• Iron velvet or other fabric onto bondaweb, cut into a strip and fold the strip evenly. Cut a pattern which touches both edges so that when you open it out, it makes a lovely repeat and apply the 'left overs' to enrich the patterns (see bottom cushion, opposite page).

Mix and match velvets with surprising contrast fabrics to gain maximum impact from its surface quality. The cushions opposite demonstrate a range of bonding methods with machine and hand stitching. The cushions are displayed on a thin cotton velvet dyed by Leslie Morgan using Procion dyes. (See 'World of Embroidery' ; Autumn 1993, p.162)

Pennie Marsden - 'Neck piece & Purse'
The fabric for both was constructed with black lace and velvet scraps bonded and machined before being enriched with beads and tassels. They are displayed on a background fabric of silk viscose devoré velvet.

Stitching to Enrich

Velvet is a delight to handle and stitch and there are numerous ways of developing the fabric so think carefully of the appropriate quality of surface or stitch to suit the purpose or idea.

Some thoughts for consideration
• Bold stitching will add vigour to a strong surface whereas subtle stitching may disappear ineffectually into the pile.
• Solid areas of machine or hand stitching will flatten the pile and add emphasis to the unworked areas thus creating exciting sculptural effects.
• Place velvet in a prepared frame and machine with a darning foot for ease of movement. (Use tissue paper over the frame to prevent spoiling the surface but don't leave the fabric in the frame longer than necessary).
• Support stretchy fabrics on cotton or calico to prevent distortion.
If distortion is desirable, work hand or machine without a frame and watch the fabric contort into dramatic contours. Bold hand stitch worked BEFORE machine stitching offers a sumptuous surface with interesting undulations.

The illustrations demonstrate some of the numerous possibilities of this lustrous fabric and could inspire you to experiment and experience at first hand the delights of voluptuous velvet.

Gwen Hedley -
'Indian Fragment' (detail)
Inspired by Indian patterning, this richly textured piece incorporates layers of fabric applied, cut back and machined with velvet exposed to add the luscious contrast.
Photography - Peter Read

Velvet/canvas sampler:
This sequential sampler shows the progression towards a richly stitched surface. Working clockwise from the top left:

• Onto acrylic painted canvas, transfer-painted synthetic velvet was bonded, cut, ironed and machined.
• Detached chain was worked over the velvet.

• Machine stitching into hand stitching gives a rich surface.
• Additional hand stitching into the ground and over the machining adds further pattern and texture.

*Sarah Westwood - Velvet Panel
Inspired by the Bayeux tapestry, a
range of contrasting, delicate
fabrics have been applied and
interlaced onto a velvet ground to
achieve a delicious texture,
enriched by machine stitch and
manipulative techniques.
Photography - Peter Read*

Above:
'Echoes' - New Zealand (detail)
A mixed media piece on linen
ground with rust, procion dyed
velvet for visual and tactile contrast.

Left :
Karen E. MacPherson - Velvet Sample
Procion dyed silk viscose velvet with
alternating blocks of machine
threads to give a chequered effect.

Suppliers

Kemtex Colours
Chorley Business &
Technology Centre,
Euxton Lane, Chorley,
Lancashire. PR7 6TE
Tel: 01257 230220
(Procion, acid dyes and
pigment colours).

Omega Dyes
Tippet's Cottage,
Kenwyn Church Road,
Truro, Cornwall
TR1 3DR
Tel: 01872 227323

Shirley Leaf & Petal Company
58a High Street,
Old Town, Hastings,
East Sussex, TN34 3EN.
Tel & Fax: 01424 427793.
(Stiffened coloured cotton
velvets designed for flowers but
which discharge and wash to
leave a silky sheen).

Fibrecrafts
(www.fibrecrafts.com)
Old Portsmouth Road,
Peasmarsh,
Guildford,
Surrey.
GU3 1LZ
Tel: 01483 565800
(Fabric paints & dyes).

Whaleys (Bradford Ltd.)
Harris Court
Great Horton
Bradford
West Yorkshire BD7 4EQ
Tel: 01274 576718.
(Discharge and silk viscose
velvets).

Art Van Go
(www.artvango.com)
The Studios,
1 Stevenage Road,
Knebworth, Herts.
SG3 6AN
Tel: 01438 814946
(Art materials, Fron Isaf threads).

Quality Colours Ltd.
30 B Evelina Road,
Nunhead, London, SE15 2DX.
(Screens pigments and dyes).

John Lewis shops usually hold a
range of velvets, depending on
fashion. They also stock the
foam backed ironing sheet and
velvet ironing mat.
Shops specialising in Indian
fabrics often hold a wide range
of synthetic, rayon or viscose
velvets, as well as silks. There are
also some amazing sequined and
embellished velvets which can
be used effectively.

Additional Reading

The Art & Craft
of Fabric Decoration
by Juliet Bawden
Mitchell Beazley, 1994

Complex Cloth
by Jane Dunnewold
Fiber Studio Press, 1996

Fabric Painting for Embroidery
by Valerie Campbell Harding
B.T. Batsford Ltd., London, 1991

The Art of the Needle
by Jan Beaney
Century, London, 1988

A Complete Guide to
Creative Embroidery
by Jan Beaney & Jean Littlejohn
Batsford, Autumn 1997

Embroidery Magazine
(published six times a year)
The Embroiderer's Guild,
Apartment 41,
Hampton Court Palace,
East Molesey, Surrey, KT8 9AU
(Excellent for current suppliers)

100 Embroidery Stitches
J.& P. Coats Ltd., Glasgow, 1989

Stitch Magic
by Jan Beaney & Jean Littlejohn
Quilters' Resource Publications /
Batsford, 1998

Vanishing Act
by Jan Beaney
Double Trouble Enterprises, 1997

Right: Joy Frey
Fabric length incorporating a range
of delicate cottons and synthetics
with machine and hand stitching.
The velvet highlights add weight
and visual contrast.

And Finally...

Armed with a range of beautiful samples, there are various opportunities open to you.
a. Place them in a box and put them in a cupboard.
b. The more worthwhile option is to organise them into a recipe and samples folder (An A5 ring-binder is ideal). This could also contain useful addresses and contacts.
c. The Samples may be cut up and used in panels or practical items. Simple mosaics often work very well when bonded and applied to a sympathetic background. There are examples of this on previous pages.
d. With the addition of either machine or hand stitch it is possible to make small and delicious greetings cards.

Continue to experiment with combinations of surface by using oil paint sticks, metallic permanent paints, heat transfer foils or even dimensional paints to add to your growing repertoire.

Many of these techniques could be superficial, unless used with sensitivity and this can be achieved with practice. Using relatively simple equipment, and a measure of enthusiasm, voluptuous velvets are possible.

Acknowledgments
Velvet is difficult to photograph well and many thanks are due to Michael Wicks for his skill and patience.
My thanks also go to Hannah Littlejohn and Paul Lavelle for their invaluable contributions.
Design & Production:
Jason Horsburgh
Printed By Gemini Press Limited.

Left:
Elizabeth Hinkes - Door Curtain
Applied and embroidered felt motifs onto viscose velvet with bleach discharge Further patterns were etched with a soldering iron.

Right:
Jean Littlejohn - 'Istron Magic Carpet' Machine and hand stitch on a velvet ground incorporating feather patterns to echo a worn Eastern carpet.